Once When Green

Once When Green

MARK IRWIN

UNIVERSITY OF MASSACHUSETTS PRESS

Amherst and Boston

Copyright © 2025 by University of Massachusetts Press
All rights reserved
Printed in the United States of America

ISBN 978-1-62534-865-4 (paper)

Designed by Jen Jackowitz
Set in Adobe Jensen Pro
Printed and bound by Books International, Inc.

Cover design by adam b. bohannon
Cover photo by Enrique Martínez Celaya, *The Enchantment*, © 2012.
Courtesy of the artist.

Library of Congress Cataloging-in-Publication Data

Names: Irwin, Mark, 1952- author.
Title: Once when green / Mark Irwin.
Description: Amherst ; Boston : University of Massachusetts Press, 2025. |
Series: Juniper Prize for Poetry
Identifiers: LCCN 2024032849 (print) | LCCN 2024032850 (ebook) |
    ISBN 9781625348654 (paperback) | ISBN 9781685751449 (ebook) |
    ISBN 9781685751456 (epub)
Subjects: LCGFT: Poetry.
Classification: LCC PS3559.R95 O53 2025 (print) | LCC PS3559.R95 (ebook) |
    DDC 811/.54—dc23/eng/20240719
LC record available at https://lccn.loc.gov/2024032849
LC ebook record available at https://lccn.loc.gov/2024032850

British Library Cataloguing-in-Publication Data
A catalog record for this book is available from the British Library.

For Lisa Utrata and Enrique Martínez Celaya,

in memory of William and Mary Lou Irwin,

and for friends—some ghosts—still close, haunting the green.

. . . Back to the body of earth, of flesh, back to the mouth, the throat, back to the womb, back to the heart, to its blood, back to our grief, back, back, back.

—*Natalie Diaz, "The First Water is the Body"*

. . . to tell what the forests
were like

I will have to speak
in a forgotten language

—W. S. Merwin, "Witness"

Contents

I   Lapsed pastoral

II   Between the edge and center

III Brief and unlasting

IV Autumnal hellos

Once When Green

I Lapsed pastoral

These things that live by perishing

1

Ago, long—ever since I left that snow-bed in another life—making
         my way down through pines and birches, toward
      the valley where those small green bodies, the first tellurians
slipped among grass, their words the *stutter, click, and whir*
         of insects—or avian *caw*

unending. And the river's sashay and hum. Keeping its sound
         alive in this poem, and the imago
of stonefly and caddis swarming, each one having burst
      its naiad shell, after all of the instars. —These things
that live by perishing through breeze and light. —Wind,

2

salt-rinse off ocean. Small steps now, as the house—the one
         on my back—becomes boat, each wave a *Yes* chorusing
     yes, yes, yes, buoying me, salt on salt. Above—gulls,
gray, quarreling air, their *ha-ha-ha-ing* at our trace
      of garbage and carbon. We—waiting—are falling faster, saith

3

the fish. —And some flowers, wept here. Afloat, I follow
         sea-cycles, the waves luminous feet, milky at night, phosphorescent
     with plankton bloom. Who am I now, all
middle, distant, dreamed? —Nascent

         sea foam, and morning cataracting light through bruised
     cumuli—theatrical their heft and pomp
enacting me—for what? My small craft now scat & feather-
        flocked. Look! One near island's green, sun-struck. —Yes,

now feathers in my ears, mouth—my body growing   porous,
    hungry.   —Just one more step,   one more toward cloud.

A day, a thousand days, and a hundred years

The blue jay that flew through the open window, fluttered about
then vanished, leaving some wildness. She too wanted that
    in her life and tried to find it in language.

Sometimes we need to say words that make us feel,
    taste, or smell—*corduroy, cinnamon, lilac*. She
recalls the smell of oregano in rain, an invisible

mountain calling forth, and how the drifting stars seem unformed
words, or that there was always a hidden blank within each sentence

    that needed to be filled in? Sometimes it hurts, this listening
close—the word *No* so filled with shadow,
    and *Yes* with its wide, slapping ocean. Time

with its long-i engine not wanting to run down. She knew it like the wind
or the haze of dust settling and resettling on the desk and bureau,

its ghost of a person, time that only slows for a moment
    of desire, or begins, making so much
unknowable like birth or the future's

inscrutable distance—a day, a thousand days, and a hundred
years, and then to feel age like the weight of a coat. She tries

    to brush a gnat off the page but then it becomes
a stain among other words. This world
    the sad or good work of our hands. The seesaw

of joy and sorrow beneath a sky that's too big and wide,
but if you were to open the house and look down there among
the moving bodies, wouldn't you see a little eternity escaping?

Weight

Tonight comet Neowise's phosphorescent tail fizzles
downward through the long drink of dark and I feel the sky
open the way it did once when a yellow kite
tore upwards blue from unsure hands. Once I watched a house's
flames burn through drifting snow and recalled how the mind ashamed
will cringe around some deed. —That man trundling through drifts, waving his arms
through the orange air while trying to avoid one exact center
which is death? Tonight, the sky's swarming so vast with stars
it seems like dawn, and those who tuck a child late into bed
will feel the heart ease through flesh. In one dream
I'm piling mother's clothes onto the bed. How much do they
weigh? I keep asking, placing one pillowcase on the scale,
and then the clothes become a mountain too soft to climb. In Noordwijk
there's an anechoic chamber whose sound-absorbing walls mimic
the silence of outer space, something now I can almost hear,
here, all-tactile, among clothes, each garment whose scent
recalls a different time, and I want so much to keep writing this ending
as I push harder and harder on a pencil that leaves no words.

Yes

Seeing the seven-hundred-year-old church bell unearthed,

its iron skirt half-rusted, the clapper gone, I imagine those notes

pealing, marking time now, buried though plowing

the silence, humus of beetle and bright maggot, and remember

my dead partner's dream, urgently told, shaking me from sleep. *There*

are those who forge the bell, molten iron in furnace heat, and those

who braid the ropes from hemp, attach them to bells and pull the ropes,

and finally those who just listen to the bells. Yes, she said, we must

learn to listen, and yes sometimes now when I dream this recounting,

although I cannot hear that music rising like mist from their giant rocking bodies,

I can see the sweaty arms wielding shadow, the hands pulling, twisting

the wet hemp, wet like her once breathing body among the breathing

of bells, which is the music I'm striving to hear in the dream

of her dream, their joinery where I'm still looking for feral words,

listening even to those stones the orange sun sometimes turns to sound.

Holiday Inn

When we checked into the hotel, I remembered how we'd been
intimate in the forest, and that love is not a fleeing into nature
but an opening, just like that attempt to get back to your
childhood room, door after door that can only lead to more trees
fuzzy with birds. The hotel was not crowded, but those bells
we heard were only the sporadic tumble of coins from a machine
vending drinks, not the vespers from that church in the mountains. We
did drive there the next day, sat in the wax-scented silence opening
the way moss will near a spring, or the slow-motion dead into our
minds. Yes, as though they are trying to reconceive, rekindle
the sparking seconds—cricket or sparrow chirp, laughter—while the house
sags in shadow, yet memory is an opening too, trying new riffs
to make things last, accessing then excessing the present briefly the way
rain does, its fecund scent summoning others, some from that childhood
room that you are approaching now, the desk drawer filled with green
acorns, the chert arrowhead, and the collection of buffalo nickels, year
by year, in the small blue folder, the buffalo out of bounds now,
the herd we saw on the way home below Spinney Mountain, twenty
or so by the fence, shaggy, their great heads snorting, tons of small
thunder, their hooves and horns, the lost root and roof of the land.

In the Arcade

I was once a real bear, at least that's what the sign says about my complete genome sequencing, how I evolved. Families are reading it now outside my vast plexiglass diorama where kids with rental control panels can make me growl or stand on my hind legs, moving my arms up and down in a Y-motion as they laugh and shout, *Disco bear, disco bear!* But during the quiet nights when the arcade's closed and river sounds play through the diorama, I'll remember romping through a May meadow of sedge grass, then splashing after brook trout in Chalk Creek. —Or cracking open a wild hive in a willow log and gorging on honey under the noon sun! How slow the days seem now! —Waiting for tokens, then the slight shock that torques my body— arms, and claws upwards—ending in a crowd-pleasing roar. Outside, behind the arcade, is a small zoo and sometimes when they open the back door, I'll glimpse and smell my former life where a brown bear mopes about in an enclosure and kids throw him pieces of fruit. How I pity that creature clinging to the old world where viewers gaze with such nostalgia. Yes, to think that before he was a wild creature unbounded! I once thought that was freedom—but how in a receding wilderness no longer mine? Now I worry that I've not escaped far enough into the future, for even a woman in a green dress summons something inside me, especially if she's standing alone in the sun.

Things I said

I said, *I know I know,* just
because I'd read it, but I didn't
know though they said I did.

I said, *I'll help you,* but I saw it
on TV and it all fell asleep
in a tall pile of images.

I said, *The springs seem slower now,*
less green, more roads, the plastic's
faster. The sulfur-air makes

it hard to breathe. The Great Pacific
Garbage Patch is twice the size
of Texas, the fish are schooling *ifs.*

I said, *Those flowers, the lilacs and irises,*
are losing their scent while on TV
perfumes keep hawking eternity.

I said, *We cheered with the Left*
over gun control while the extreme
Right rioted then stormed the Capitol.

I said, *We saw them see it, heard*
them hear it. Watched the replays
on our monitors while we were

being watched, branded. It was then
I started questioning my gender. Men
have a long history of violence.

I said to my partner, *I love you
but who are you?* because we'd
been working in separate rooms.

So long, I said. *So long,* she
said, and we both died close
by but in other countries.

Avalanche

Red blood cells
        magnified 5000 times,
frozen in their tranced

tumbling from the heart's
        forest, erythrocytes,
scarlet, sensing life—

        blond hair streaming
from a convertible, cotton
        candy torn by a mouth,

        scent of parsley after
rain, wrens chattering on
        the powerline, each

of the senses opening. Yes,
        these juxtaposed against
the live-feed of cars

drifting through the Eisenhower
        Tunnel or infrared of deer
crossing White Creek makes

you want a feral
        word—*elk*—that one
turning its rack under

ordinal stars—hooves
        over talus, clacking the way
any good consonants

will in the avalanche
  of language. A nursery
school class chanting

their *ABCs* in chorus,
  or babel of that evangelist.
I prefer eros, that other,

older red cloth
  where if lucky
sometimes we lie

blurred. The glory of those
  moments camping, pointing
toward Venus to make

ourselves unbound, as
  when I took the wrinkled,
reaching hand of that

chimpanzee in mine
  and we both looked
woken from a spell.

What if ?

To become this iris waiting to be ungowned
as the warm spring breezes come. Now feelings
of arriving are confused with departing. You wish to leave
but have no place to go, for place is changing
everywhere. The forsythia's sulfur-yellow boughs lit with twitching bees,
blackbirds nesting, chirping, flashing their chevrons through the hedgerows, and frogs
grunting among cattails in the marsh. Now you would like to become free enough
to fill the moments beginning to occur. Last night in sleep
the seeds you planted became small blue flames that grew taller. What
fruit might they bear? What if this life
is just the porch to something else? What if that bee slowed
by frost on the autumn sill is just waiting for the light
to become the exact length to open its body?

Pause

In the dream, mother—dead—is waiting to give birth
to me, but I, sixty years later, am waiting to die.
It's the terrifying patience that wakes me—hers, mine, ours—
and I begin painting a landscape, mixing blue into red
more and more until the violet of dusk goes muddy
with dark. In that dream we are both sitting, looking
at each other in a room that becomes a field expanding
between us with the seasons—spring greening, summer's
lull, fall's yellows and clove, winter's white streaming,
and then we are back in the room, staring at each other
like strangers whose unknown love is ripening. This
is when I wake just as she says, *Don't worry*, but I do,
for her, us, who still have to build a house made of
feeling as it becomes unbearably bright at the dream's
end, which is memory coursing back, accepting all
the new seconds, each one lit, opening, then closing a life.

Less Vast Pastoral

If the question is about distance, the answer
is receding forests. If the question's about time,
we are falling and risk having
only memory. Yes, we are moving forward, following
the sun but—as when driving the same roads—
remember the future. How to become explorers, cartographers
again. We are lapsed tellurians and that one cloud,
elbowing the mountain, reminds. *Come,*
the mountain says. *Come inside.* Its blunt steeple
resisting time. Its caves that enclose
the body. The hours know
the body, the years the mind. We breathe, and then
vanish. How to become
more? Blood, carbon, star, leaf. —To reach where the present
opens chance, and verbs sail, crisscrossing
through words, where the horns of those deer
taper into that mountain whose creeks are finding a river, a first
language, a home, a thirst for listening.

Fast

          Our bodies over which the seconds fling as red blood cells
      form within marrow, or the one-celled
phytoplankton that reproduce by dividing and go on, phosphorescent,

to shine. —In a poem, the pockets of time between verb, comma, and event
      when a meadowlark's trill rises, then holds over an entire April
field, its alfalfa, while bricks—within a century's gray—
          crumble, or pixels on a blue screen

          collapse. *Goodbye*, I shouted over the open
      threshold's gap, and the one between touch. *How fast
the flesh*, daffodils lining the drive, then her ashes

three months later—now thirty years—fingerprints on a doorjamb, and some
      dandelions, their globed heads dusk-filled around a grave.

Gap

The sudden space between us and him, the boy dressed in camo, waving

a semi-automatic weapon, spraying bullets into the holiday crowd,

wounding several before being tackled by a half-costumed Santa, but right before

the gap closed between us, the pistol he waved became knife, the mall just a clump

of trees on the prairie where we were settlers, then the knife became a stone

in the hand of someone having taken unrightful claim to a cave,

overlay after overlay tumbling back, centuries, but I swear when the five wounded

fell, those baubles—on the Christmas tree by the fountain—dropped and became

apples, soft mealy apples, and people stared at them, their faces lit

with a blush-red like those bystanders outside in the parking lot's strobing lights

where a thick frost fell and continues to fall like snow, deep as it is fine.

II Between the edge and center

Here I am again,
working between the edge and center,

trying to mend what matters. On the edge
it was the pronghorn caught in barbed wire—whose head
I held while a friend worked pliers
on the tight-strung thigh. Those small hinges—and the eyes'
wild fear before it sprang, its full *geste*
of being in wind, like fire or rain you can see
right through, that kind of being, that kind of life let loose.

But the center's much harder, as when you say to a dying person,
"I am here," and that "I" is a bridge. —Or that arrowhead
found in situ with human teeth before
snow, a page we could then all write on with the weight
of our entire bodies. At noon I wear
the dead man's hat and there is no shadow but mute *hello*.

And the fossil shape bird beaks have pecked
into the salt block resembles pinnacles and cairns until there
is nothing but white, flattened the way an elephant's face appears
like an ancient shield set before the eyes, caved
within whorls, a geography one cannot attain, a ruin for gazing.

Wind

When the one dying, who had carried me within her
body, said, *We grow into the night as*

    into a jacket that fits perfectly, and as you
button it up, the hours and years, the seconds continue
    to glitter past, and saying that, she gestured

toward my father's blue cashmere jacket, and I could feel
    it tugging me like a hook, and she continued, *the naming of things*
will end just as the alphabet, and putting her arm

    around my neck, we stared into the future, and the moments
streaming like sparks stung our faces, and the earth blushed under the big red sun.

While someone sings the blues

If, when you begin to write, blood seeps from your hand, will you continue?
If, when you read aloud what you'd written, your teeth begin to ache,
will you continue? Outside the window

cattle graze on the tall June grass. We write the red book with our bodies,

and how the red book fits inside the green one we call life.
We should draw deep maps across the country
to know how the dead became dead, just as we have tall monuments

telling how the living became famous—birth-jacket to president or CEO—

then each gives a farewell long as autumn, but here where the cattle hunger on,
we live on sidereal time so that when the stars come round again
to the same place, we call it a night and sleep well for that is a part of the same

book where birds fly from buried tree to tree, their scarlet plumage in vivid detail.

Reckless to the Point of Elegance

The way any star-shaped object explodes the pupils outward,
the way I touch angles of sleeping bodies, some still
living, others receded far into the years'

slow-motion spaces. Pinyon jays—tearing blue—parachute
among pines. A squawking and chattering among limbs
reminds of the wild hallelujahs at First Pentecostal

Church where outside Gatlinburg a coral snake was passed
hand to hand. —God, a verb. Relentless,
sweating, they sang.

Zooming in on the Crab Nebula's fibrous orange-green
reef of light, one glimpses the wobbly blue-glow
thrown out by spiraling

electrons of the collapsed neutron star, one tablespoon of which
would outweigh Mount Everest. While finishing his
last painting, *Study of a Bull*, Francis

Bacon dragged the half-dry work through the dust of his studio
floor. The work shows a ghostly creature exiting
a black void into the white

glare of two panels, one horn visible in each. Bacon said
that he would like his paintings "to look as if
a human being had passed

between them like a snail leaving its trail." The neutron star's
spectacular death—in the constellation Taurus—spews
a blizzard of particles, debris,

light, which creates the nebula. When the red and yellow coral snake
was handed past me, the flickering tongue
registered a babel of scents,

voices in excelsis like that orange cloud of bees around
a rotten log while the blue barn swallows,
chirping, clucking, veered—beaks open—

through the porous body of hum. —The swooping blue and swarming
gold, vivid with loss as a Giotto fresco, Apriled
with green in the churching air.

A Swarm of Patience

I'm always in a hurry like the wind, or those daffodils blabbing yellow through spring snow. When others walk through a field, I'll run, saying, "Hey, c'mon" to the sheep and moseying cows. I'm in a hurry, like when you're hungry, but I'm not. "Hey," I'll say on the first date, "I love you," and feel the freefall through language. *Abracadabra*, I'll often say to myself, urging something new. Alone, working at home, often I'll open and close doors, pretending to arrive or go! I'm kind of like a paramedic, running toward the emergencies I create or imagine. Once, sitting in a café, I told two men, *I love you* and *you*, then ran after each. All my life I've been hurrying till my mother was dying. "Sit still," she said, and by God I did. Noon and we were alone in her bright room. "I'm sorry," I said. "Shh," she said loudly, and then I repeated it, *Shh*, more quietly. We went on this way, face to face in a long game and then there was just the wind moving on to the next place.

October

Far into a deciduous forest I found a knight asleep

in his armor, muddy and tarnished. Groggy, he

asked about his horse though I saw none, only

a torn blue saddle blanket embroidered with yellow

crosses, some mealy apples, and a splintered lance

that more resembled a child's rusty dart. The evening light,

everywhere gold, seemed to rouse an ardent tone in his speech.

He had a small cut by his mouth and the bleeding made

his words more urgent. Perhaps because I'm a mother

of kids now grown, it moved me that he desired something

far away so desperately, and that long in the past.

It

is a bridge, its
words suspended over space and time, a sentence
forking like lightning, feeling its way from sky to earth
and then back again. Dying,
she said to the one once carried within her body, "Here is the key to the cabin
where you were born," and a year after the funeral
he drove there with a grief which, upon seeing the crib and blanket
embroidered with his name, turned to joy.

It is a river, an accumulation of other voices distilled into one.
People are standing above it, talking or listening.
It is a mountain that by climbing people come to believe
not what they've left but what they
have at that moment as they turn
through the new seconds, standing on air.

Map

In dream a monkey approached and held out a branch

with small green leaves, so sudden, there was daylight. I reached

out to take it but she held on, then let go while looking with rheumy eyes. She

took my free hand and looked into its palm, running her black

finger there, then I took her palm. It was pinkish-black, deeply creased.

I looked far into its deep map while she, with her free hand,

pulled my face down into its humus scent. This is when I woke,

walking out into the long June light. It was morning but seemed

like evening the way the light fumed around crowns of trees

reaching toward sky, trees reaching toward one another across the earth.

Look,

the Mexican man playing an accordion, leaning against the back of his Ford Explorer
with his six-year-old daughter who smiles in a sunflower dress when given
five dollars and looks at her father, smiling too, gracious over
a sign asking for food or money for a hotel room. The Mexican man named
Jorge who turns a Colorado strip mall into a street on the Left Bank
of Paris with his playing as Luisa, his daughter, dances and bows
to the lilting music. To be this man and girl made entirely of music
and sunlight. Made of giving more than wanting.
To live inside that girl's smile when her father kisses her goodnight
in the back of their SUV as he tucks her in between bags of food and water bottles.
Look, she's curtsying now, leaning into him till they are one
swaying body filled with desire without object except to subsist and dwell
safely. If there is a mother, the father has become her, wearing that aura
of care. Their beauty seeps through the music in waves, their happiness resurrecting
the faces of harried shoppers, tired figures lofting like bees
toward something sweet, a music making me clumsy with purpose. This evening
they will camp by the river whose gold light will make their bodies and faces
invisible while a radiance surges through the full current of their lives.

Shared

The March breakfast at the nursing home, our last, your spoon

slipped, breaking a yolk—ketchup on your lip—as you recalled

the honeymoon, Niagara Falls, its midsummer mist rising while

outside, a red squirrel leapt from one branch to another, snow

dislodged. We seemed like an iceberg split slowly apart, then I

an explorer returned, looking for one wild word to take with me,

one to net the years, youth still in your laughter reminding that you

were a daughter, then wife. The gold Elgin watch given to him after

24 monthly payments now on my wrist, you dozing off as the server

pours coffee, sugar spilled there—& oh the pink cotton candy we shared

once, faces bent in a stiff wind, time opening those moments their words.

Toward

Late at night when time is cut by sleep and you can feel lives passing.
Andrew always kept a fire pre-made in the woodstove. —Liver
spots on a face demolished by time I can't forget as a tiny
red spider scurries across this page. Toward what

threshold will you move? A lock's tumbler turns, the planets
spin, accelerating the motion of motion, and sometimes the earth
splits apart and you must take a giant step, and sometimes in winter

I'll make a tower of snow where once I'd fallen, or tripped
while touching another body, and where that tower
melts in spring will always be a forest and white pulp turning toward
page where I'll feel very close to something I can only

touch with words, as when sitting with Jeanne
on a waterbed in our first apartment, how she kept giggling, slowly
bouncing with its waves till we fell into one another's arms,
unwieldly—a great freedom and restraint like that.

For luck

In the park someone crafts a giant head made from a sheet
stuffed with other sheets and mounts it on the hill with a pole.
Long ropes hang like hair from the head and whenever anyone dies,
someone's family comes and ties a knot in one rope. After many
years, each rope has many knots and people travel far to touch
these limp, coiled forms for luck. —Large and small hands alike reaching
to touch. Someone spray-paints the head green one day, and the next month
another brushes yellow spikes so that it appears the head wears a crown.
The image grows famous and travelers are seen with its image tattooed
on their arms. Ceremonies are held on the grass around it at dusk
till one March day a homeless man's found dead there, beaten and tied up
with the knotted ropes, and that morning the river—running through the park—
stops. Birds, mid-flight, freeze in the air. People abandon their ceased cars
on the street, and single file they come toward that torn, stuffed head,
each pressing a face close, just once, or ever again in sleep.

How long, how bright?

Waking to hands all over my face, each one giving everything, nothing.

          —The hawk, high, gliding through a thermal, turning above
where its mate was killed on the powerline. Without

                                  falling, how marvelous this world
where *hello* means how long, how bright? Speckles of blood
on a wedding dress where her nose bled at the waterfall. She blinked

                           then the children were grown, her parents
shuffling through the dusk. Or how you could say each sleep is a partial shadow,
     building a far horizon we try to describe in words
          that continue to fail, except *green* still opening its sound

                in winter's keening light, the difficult becoming
more beautiful. Kathleen Battle holding the "a" in *Hallelujah*, or that giraffe
       reaching its tongue through thorns for acacia leaves at dawn.

Going

Mother, draped in black on the basement stairs, that's how
      I found her, getting off my bike, approaching
home in the dark, opening a series of doors to her
      there. What's wrong? I asked, thinking it was my father's
death. She looked up through the stratums of shadow, pitch—smiled,
      then spoke in a language of whisper and slur I could only
feel, not know. When her father died, to soothe her mother,
      Marie, she asked me to go kiss Grandpa George, and I did,
running like an athlete from the sidelines to the coffin, placing
      my lips on his cold cheek. Now, looking into Mother's face
I'm looking into a well, its channeled dark gathering
      water's far trickle—voices of other dead—where a glint
holds diminished sky. Why? She seems to ask, holding up
      a white thumb whose prick of blood lights for a moment
all the hours, years—its call colored like the firetruck her
      father drove, its red going scarlet, carmine, rouge, coral—
a tiny flag, kerchief, windless save in the spring of our minds.

III Brief and unlasting

Across

When the rain in sunlight began that afternoon and swallows
        swooped the shallow air for insects, there was a light
you could not touch but see gaining within the green,
        something like seconds becoming minutes and hours
unending, the wet pine needles sharpened in brightness while fry
        dimpled the creek's surface and the lupine steepened their violet
all into evening where a web, each of its filaments shone,
        and if—like the spider—we could step into the middle of air,
not taking a life, but giving one over and over, then we
        might feel that wind of forever as the new light begins
vanishing, only the scent of chlorophyl still opening
        there in the dark while I spoke the word *yesterday* with great
sorrow as clouds like ghost-ponds kept floating across the sky.

Brief and unlasting

—Brief and unlasting like the iris' flag unfolded, enthralling
      with rain-scent and mutable violet, or the seeming violent-
in-swiftness that builds when the fertilized egg divides—zygote,
      morula, to blastula—the berry-shape becoming hollow in divisional
detail, as when a star begins to form, the dense molecular cloud
      congealing within nebula. Through telescopes we've glimpsed
their creation towers, ladders reaching through green fire, climbing
      toward a farther light. —Or solar flares, their massive coronal eruptions,
this beauty in creation and destruction. So too in language when
      Homer describes Meriones' arrow point piercing Adamas' groin
till he falls: "And the black blood flowed and the ground was wet with it."
      Or in Bosnia, the Dutch soldier fleeing with an infant during
the genocide, the barbed and feathering seconds streaming at once. So too in
      April, the fire asleep in each tree but summoning us with green.

Window

The general stares at a combat screen. In a wrist's
turn a hundred will perish, and upon that outdoor faucet's
forming drop of water you can see a school's collapsed

walls and Russian tank approaching. A mother shushes
her crying baby in the bathroom where a small crack
in the plaster forms before the HE round explodes,

killing twenty while the wounded feel for cover or try
to speak with mouths that have found moans
instead of words, and what are they compared to blossoming

screams? The cup of coffee about to be made where the kitchen's
now half-gone, but her baby's *alive*—crying—the blood on
the tiny fumbling hand her own. Dust settling through blanketed

sunlight, a fly suturing halves of air, buzzing some code against one
unbroken window, and sooty clouds clumped above bodies on the ground.

Blueprint for Survival Found after a Future War

Now one of the human soldiers makes his way home to the mountains, hoping
his mother and father are still alive. Walking into the dusk valley, he

sees there among the elfed trees, their house, becoming smaller and smaller
as he approaches—their house once his house—the tiny windows

butter-lit, his mother there in the kitchen, humming, doing the dishes,
his father on the couch, reading the paper in a cone

of light, and peering into one window, trying to see into his own once-room,
he can hear the toilet running like a distant creek, and—yes—now he can see

there on the shrunken wall, a map, not with states, but the one for
his life, the green threaded rivers leading toward people, the threads

fraying, and he wants to tug each thread, and now recognizing
the tune his mother is humming, he would like to lean

way down and tie his father's shoe so he might not trip
in age, pet his dog Rocket graying by the muzzle, clear the past's corridors

of light disrupted by the TV's news feed—danger? —if only he could
gather them in his hand, but even that's too big so he tries to loosen

the house but, when tilting it just a bit, sees the green veins
binding it to earth start to bleed, and he realizes, yes, that he must leave

before they go to sleep, so he breathes lightly through the chimney—
the lamp light brightening—turns, never so happy and walks back over the hill.

Between

In life I was chasing a deer. In sleep the deer
was chasing me. In life I was climbing a mountain.
In sleep I was a tree, a pine among many pines in wind.
A friend's lying down there now under the dry needles.
In life I was swimming across the warm lake in June.
In sleep I was under a rock, a tadpole turning into

a frog. In sleep I gave the homeless man
a burrito. In life they kicked him into a ditch
then beat him with rebar. In sleep I'm stepping through
mist into an ocean's brine. In life I'm watching its
waves uncurl through pixels on an iPad's screen.
Angry, sometimes it's hard to sleep till in life
we find beauty in small details. Life and sleep seem close
until when awakening all the senses close.

for Angie Estes

Astronaut

Late in the life of our planet and having failed at love, I've been
sent into space for a month. Nothing fancy, just orbiting the moon,
which my doctor says will be good for my condition, looking
at its gray seas and craters, along with the solitude of looking back
at our own blue and green sphere, auraed in pollution, stubborn and still
bristling with life. What I recall now is the snow-light through winter's
skeletal trees, the fur of dusk, the bee that stung me at mother's funeral,
which made love come flooding back, and *here,* this gray feather, Pip's,
my pet pigeon eaten by a fox. How its grenadine eyes—amidst cooing—
shown in sunlight! Being an astronaut is often like being dead, the blackness
of space continual save for the faint fires we call nebulae and the small
light of stars. Little changes and I become more aware of how love relies
on changes in time—Velvet, our black Lab's gray around the muzzle,
and, on the wall of the sunroom, my deceased wife's red canvas shoes now
faded pink. I think back to when love was new and the great sense
of freedom, and now it's only those distant prickling lights
opening through the darkness of space that remind.

Warren of the dead

So many copies of numbers multiplying like minnows
that help us die, unlike when among lightning
our hearts leapt and our teeth spoke
sparks and we saw for the first time the mullein flowering
yellow and the green chain of moments, the trunks of maples
over centuries turning to coal. I am so
lonely for the present, while the next text is chirping
on a phone. I am so lonely for peace, not the tumbled walls in Gaza, torn
bodies, and unraveling DNA. I am so lonely for a river's one rushing
minute with scuttling crayfish, nymphs, and eddies blurring clouds, not its
imaged thousand pixels changing colors toward forms
on a screen. I am lonely for the swallows riding a canyon's
thermal far from a helicopter's blades slapping air through smog, and far
from the numbers written within passwords securing
our nameless names.

Et in Arcadia Ego

Once as a kid he'd buried a pet rabbit in that meadow,
now they're building a new subdivision of twenty houses
but so far just the foundations have been poured so that from the hill
the site resembles a series of giant graves. —And once he ran
across that space, a kite tugging his arm. Age of the body, age of the land
where 150 million years ago brontosauruses roamed. They swallowed
stones to help digest their food, stones still littering that field,
brontosauruses still lingering as the green icon on Sinclair Oil signs
across the land while here, where a bulldozer ploughs a new road,
an articulation of crows in the crown of a dead elm—tribunal
for the way we've come—their *caw, caw, cawing* sounds half lullaby,
half scherzo. My friend Diane says the beauty of the world is there
because it hurts. Geronimo refusing to surrender, then finally sequestered
to Florida. He, who'd roamed his native land, locked up in another. Here
in this field, a few dried-up puffballs, each one containing trillions of spores,
a black dust the air finds. Brief diaspora, near or far, depending on wind.

In the wind

In wind we are living. What is it telling us with all its breaths and stories?
        With all its beginnings and ends? What will you tell and how far
will those words travel to the page? The man who carried

        me on his shoulders is dead. Wind where we fished
on the river, wind through mountains, then the fires we made, talking
        words across flames lobbing shadows from our faces till sleep's

black breeze, till we drove home the next day and he would open
        all the windows, watching the newspaper and magazine pages fly, and outside
someone would scream, and inside someone would whisper, and that's what

        poetry is, I think, the immediacy of scream, or urgency
of whisper, perhaps over an urn wherein there's no
        wind. —To witness a world that is perishing—the frogs,

pandas, and drought-stricken trees. The salamanders, manatees, and wolves. How
        will we name their ghosts, abbreviating our lives? Their pictures
haunting the internet. Will you become a bridge to save them? —Like

        the man who burns his small boat on shore when the fish
are gone—the bluegill and bass—and then disappears into the whistling
        trees, then into a city's streets where he sleeps in a box
                —a bridge like that, blowing apart.

Tomorrow

This morning the wind and light arriving from the same direction
where the man on his heels leans into it—blinks, helmeted
for his destiny. He needs a car—to be enclosed in stuttering traffic.
He needs to move toward his new living pod, his debt-
load, his wasteland, but the meadowlark's trill says, *listen.*
The rusted tractor says, *wait,* while the spangled ponds wink
their ancient codes, but he tires of their continual refrains. He tires
of his name John, and would like to be called Neon, Astro, or Tomorrow.
He tires of the names of things. I'll have 3 of #721, please.
He likes being in an elevator, watching the numbers illumine, before
stepping out onto the observation deck's winged view of those gridded
buildings. He could be looking down at a circuit board or a game
of Monopoly. Now he thinks of the babies, all of them, and of those
yet to be born, lined up, crying behind him. Toted here and there,
they are the long will of others. That's why they're crying—why we
still begin crying at times. —The memory of being dragged by the future.
These country roads finding concrete highways, the highways pulled
toward skyscrapers and high-rises—their inhabitants looking down
at us now, our swaying, leaning bodies wanting to climb and be whole.

Flight

It was when the coin she loved and the buffalo on
the coin began bleeding that she thought she'd cut herself,
smearing the red, but the Indian on the other side was bleeding too
as she ran toward the mountain and the prairie below where
the real buffalo ran, making clouds on the earth
joining clouds on the mountain but now the mountain was
burning and the pines, their flames crowning, resembled
blood above her horse whinnying at pasture and together
they rode toward the city through suburbs past the Burger & Mattress
Kings past the Chuck E. Cheese where the shooter had fired—
Yes, needing to rest she stopped at a school to tether
the horse next to a playground horse, a yellow pony spring-rider,
as the schoolkids, bell-cheeked and sweaty, stared hard
at the woman's horse making grass beget grass among the concrete
and jungle gym's steel bars silhouetted by the mountain's nimbus of fire.

Half-prayer

Digging my hand, my right hand into the wet loam
up to the wrist. Still I can almost move each finger, one
touching a stone, another a root the way I've touched words. The earth
cool to touch with all its minerals and microspores. Now up
to the wrist. To stop for a moment—desire,
grasp. *Look,* a deer in the woods. Our gazes lock, its front hooves
braced in the caliche. Earth, air too between us,
motes floating in sunlight—ferns. My body
attached. Hand half-prayer
to earth. My body wick to this hand, green summer
body, red autumn body, curling brown body. Hello-hand,
goodbye-hand, you must open all the doors, even
the hidden ones before giving
everything away.

Revenant

The new grass in spring, fine from seed. A FedEx

truck comes by, blows it all one way, making this

grass seem stuck the way a chimp seems stuck

within a zoo's pasteled veldt—or bee on a grape snow cone. Mom,

now dead, would say, "When are you coming home?" Ghost

of her—mint on a hot summer day. "Don't be *a lazy bones.* Wash

the car." —Over there, a homeless woman on Spring Street, Los

Angeles, with infant crying, sits in a U-Haul wardrobe

box, the frame, of sorts, made me think of Olan Mills, our family

portraits, fake smiles, bright clothes for the Black & White

pic. Licorice treat for the kids. Each *flash,* *flash* wherein I

was an explorer of time paused. April revising earth—leaves. On

my knees I wanted to tear up new grass with my teeth.

Book

I want to write the book that comes undone and flies apart
like snow through the last pages because we all move around
through spaces as time passes, the wind blowing about our
hands and through the tenses of our lives. I want to start
the book with the word *now*, the only word with open
doors, windows of *when* and *will be* because entropy
is the difference between our future and past. I want the book
to be filled with prepositions leading into open spaces,
yes, and the book must be white because time is gray
while the words stain those pages, and the book must be all one
sentence meandering, and the sentence will have roots spreading from
each word and out of the book a great tree will grow whose
spring and autumn are one, greening buds and yellow
leaves going ruddy then brown at once through the swarming
cloud of snow, sunlit, its nascent pages lost with the names of all you love.

IV Autumnal hellos

What is desire?

As when listening to a story, children always want to know
the next thing before sleep until they wake and the morning becomes
ancient, so too those beginning at love first ask, Is it real?—and then years later,
Was it a memory?—only to stare at a vast middle growing, opening
at their feet, the river of language. To be awakened to each word's
minnow-pulse, the salt-scent of human
noise, breath, texts, old letters—the rapids and eddies of stories,
poems. The three words of a dead father's faded
ink kept folded inside a wallet: *Giving is having*, the divided
trochees' out-breath unending. The bird flying within each of us
whose wings are hands, the hands of words joining people,
ages in a sentence growing toward its end, leading
toward the next one in a brief waking like youth—the day and night of the page, what
keeps us moving. What is desire if not to open as the river opens
the land, words the mind of light—what keeps on
flickering in memory? The one who birthed me—long ago—hanging
sheets on the line, her body white-draped, arms still reaching out, an eclosion
holding the moment. Yes, or as Levinas says, "The excess over the present
is the life of the infinite." The way she held so much light,
then carried it in her arms, moving through the field of time
toward the house. *Toward* and not to be
without like the nomad. The sheets still a bit
damp so they might continue to grow through that night, the sound of rain
opening my sleep and into hers longer, while
jonquils and daffodils—in excelsis—burst through the green.

When it happened

When it happened you were alone or, if with someone else, you
stepped outside. There was the sound of people talking
but you heard nothing, for it had happened as it will

happen to others, earlier or later, close by or far away,
but because it happened now, you look off into the distance

where someone's writing a word in the snow, pulling, dragging
a stick through each of the giant letters, but from the distance
below that hill, the word's not legible.

Some believe the word is *Yes*, and that it contains all the words
and the ache in each of their ecstasies. Others say the word
is *No*, the origin of silence from which all words come.

You want to discover that word, but while you're approaching, the snow
begins to melt, fields green, and the word disappears.

Some say our fears keep us from knowing, for the word
is both our permission and disaster, while others say
that the melting itself is the word, a word that can only be felt,

never seen. Yet we all wait and are left
only with that waiting, the waiting that is language's opening,
and we stare hopelessly at one another as though we were made of words.

Tinder

All this time I've been waiting for the kindling to become
dry, the shower of sparks lofting against
green. It's no different when one fluent in silence
speaks. The fire builds, I speak louder, adding fatwood till flames

drown those words. One way to strengthen wood while building
a boat is to char it lightly. One way to strengthen love is to leave,
then return—the way words leave then return

with memory. Right now I'm speaking to no one—I'm stepping
into the boat. The boat is a kind of movable
bridge like a name, a means to approach through language
where verbs light the way. They are the wind too

that sets things a-sail. Verbs that open. And the light and pollen
inside, spreading across the page, your leaning
face, you with a name, a name opening like a room

so others may enter, a room that one day will empty, but if we
could step into language after the things it names
are gone, how strange when memory becomes desire. As when you say

a dead lover's name and smell the salt, sun-scented skin. The rage
of spring. Rain, bees, forsythia—each branch a sulfur-colored blossoming fuse.

Living vessel

As when the dead come back in sleep and you grasp
at the lit erasure leaving its wake in memory, and then
walk to the kitchen, run the tap, drinking water, still thirsty,
remembering when they all were alive, reaching across
the table for butter, their faces pink from the steaming corn,
the tenor of voices rising and falling in conversation, lulls
then rushes, as when listening to that river from a distance,
you decided to wade into the swift current, its living
vessel through earth, and in the shallows picked up
a stone and glimpsed inside that stone a mountain, yes
& there in a small pool the salamanders—swirling,
touching—changing colors to display emotion, so much
more honest you thought, and wished you could call those
loved ones back, the numbers in their ages, or words trying
to fray back into letters, the letters into sounds, then brief
flesh, a flash through neurons triggering scent or the exact tone
of speech, and you want suddenly to clap like those children
who by doing so bring the dead back to life, though instead we're left
with their furniture, rugs, photos, clothes, and the rings
that when worn conclude a secret pact to be passed down,
but what I remember most are the two of us by the stream, him
teaching the child how to fish, the trout's gold-green body
speckled red—quaking in hands—that coursed and was gone.

The time it took

She's seven and I want
        to show her
a sunflower taller than
        she is in a field
of hundreds, early
        autumn, the slant sun
speaking my age, she
        much more dear than
this one's spangly
        crown burnished with
seeds, huge thimble
        our thumbs touch what
the past frost browns,
        making the sun
gleam more in mornings—
        what is this thing we
call death, but what
        has grown too detailed,
particular, and must
        be leveled out by
coming days and so I
        lift *you* up, your face
now the sun looking
        down into one's ragged
corolla where an old
        bee slow-hectors a rusted
petal as the real sun
        still warms, a magic
wand, but warning too
        how brief its light's
journey, one hundred
        million miles in eight
minutes, the time it
        took to lift a crimson

worm, wriggling on
      the flooded walk, then
place among the new lashes
      of greening spring grass.

Black & White Family Photograph

A Saturday afternoon in April and we've driven
the black 1957 Ford Fairlane 500 to Olan Mills Studio for our portrait.
Mother, son, father. We make a right triangle in seated height.
Mom with permed hair and wearing a navy dress, me sporting a tennis
sweater, and Dad in his blue blazer with striped tie.
We smile like fools, middle-class, middle-of-the-road folks, hard
workers always striving. Mom had cut her hand just before while chopping carrots
and smells of blood. The scent from a big dandelion in my right pocket
lingers. Outside that past space there is sun, greening, and outside too, beyond
my painting, this photo I've enlarged to life-size and continue
working only in grays, now that Mom & Dad have used up their bodies. I think of my painting
not as a flat surface but as a cave within which I'm pushing memory as light,
so that the cave is a luminous one, though leaking light.

—Painting over our slant dimensions on the wall, remembering that the area of our lives
equals the *space and time* through which our bodies have moved,

I've come to understand the approach to painting
not as a dog barking, but as a cat sleeping who occasionally wakes,
licking itself, then others. What I'm saying is that the dandelion
in my then-pocket has become a lion, hungry for the blood on mother's finger,
so I'm bordering my painting with faint, red chalk. —Look at their faces!
Mother's does not know that her father will die soon. Father's—that he will be
fired, and mine the regret of moving again. Faces stilled but moving.
The act of painting, as with people, is about touch, and most of what I touch
is missing—that magic box we called house, and what makes house
a home is that we have room for others, for love to grow wide, and now
our invisible beds grow longer and abut the walls, and though the windows
melt, and the doors sway loosely in wind, we have nowhere to go.

Three ways

The way those towers once   prodded clouds
    describes the memory of   loss. How
what's missing can have no   referent, and we
    are no longer able to call   to one
another from the arsenal   of language
    till we become our   own new echo.

* * *

The way our dead are to be desired   in a twilight
that keeps   diluting but never finds
darkness is why I   keep some
twine, a knot for each one in my   jacket pocket
where I'll pull as though   climbing upwards, my
fingers stinging. The way   their bodies did
goodness, going inside one   another to make more.

* * *

The way our   *way* will become   theirs. —Remembering
how   the sheep went one
way, the river   another. To be able
to see the turning   point of things. When
I found   her asleep on   an open
suitcase of clothes, she   woke thirsty. *Yes,* & how   the glass she
drank from—   empty, keeps filling   with light.

Luna

Considering a bridge's
        span and therein
its beauty too, I was

equally astonished
        by the vivarium
of you, the root-silk

of skin faced with
        rhino and blepharo-
plasty wrapped

in a Cleopatra-
        do, each hair
placed, and what I would

detail to those surgeons
        now is your leaping
from the Marina

del Rey balcony
        toward these kept
ashes that sometimes in

breeze cohere to
        the chitinous scales
of a luna moth's wing.

White

The way wind can go on writing nothing so perfect through snow,

moving the silence a bit more each day, moving the white

seconds, and if you believe that even in shadow's

quarrel, there's light, and that light begets

light—wind raging through hydrangeas—then that woman

among the billowing sheets, where she and her deceased once slept,

that woman, pawing their kited folds from the line, turns, becomes

dizzy and knows—beneath the scudding clouds—blindfolded with April life.

Bridge

On the tide's receding lip, plankton and sea worms
twitch, pitching phosphor into
sound while fish school, recording
the last light. How to do this with
language? "Hold me," she said, after losing
the baby. My arms a corral around diminishing
fences within whose center
was a well where I would often lean, listening
to the O's descending rings while she began
building something slender out of wood
growing tall. I think it was an ark
for words. Years later I still hear the air
of her scream—that of an almost mother's
weather she lived within. Language survives
us, a bridge we keep building toward dissolving
shores. Yes, I held her. How yellow
her blouse, yellow as a ripening fruit. We were
in the middle of our lives, but time
seemed old as those October flowers' last
flares to another world, orange zinnias turning
brown. What is the grammar of color? The past
tense of red? The future perfect of blue? Slowly we become
the shape of what we name. —Constellations in the black
sky's well. You could feel small puffs of wind
like footsteps from a name.

Date

The faucet dripping like his worry, Mom & Dad out to dinner, the babysitter trying
to distract his seven-year-old mind with jacks, checkers, marbles, Monopoly, and then
the summer constellations—Lyra, Cygnus, Scorpio—when in dark the Ford Fairlane
whose headlights he could tell from all the others, that twin beacon begins to rise over
the hill—and there it is and he's almost giddy, light-headed, running up the gravel drive,
tripping as the sitter says, "Get back in bed," but he is in bed, 60 years later, and they are
both gone, the pillow on the floor, he gets up, *yes*, the faucet dripping—water has so many
voices, their faces so clear through the windshield, and outside his window the forest that
grew overnight beneath nebulae, the chalk of childhood still trailing from his wrist as he'd
reached for her in that house where no bodies are. —Home, what is it? A door you keep
trying to make larger and keep opening, where *being* fills with time. —A hand, its soft palm.
The black Lab's spittle all over your face, then just a shadow surfacing through that maple's
light. *Yes*, just to be in it, up to your neck in life.

Incarnadine

To qualify your absence I can only paint its
red in sunlight, morphing from a carmine shade each morning
toward scarlet by noon, then progressing to a darker
rhubarb, perhaps claret by sunset, despite my efforts
to lighten its maroon, brooding by nightfall
so I keep painting, recalling your coral
nail polish, your lipstick, the one we bought in Paris
a kind of *rouge-nu*, or color of a female
cardinal—and when you nicked your thumb
on the corkscrew, mixing that in too, or when I bit your lip
and you bit mine, the iron taste of your insides become outside
is why I cannot finish the painting of you being gone.

The Cakes

When I think of them all set on different tables, each one

seems a prayer to something lost, all of us making wishes, small

wind among small fires, our faces right there, each cake the head of someone

unrecognizable the dark might reveal, our own insecurities too,

and as we begin eating now, this one resembles something partially excavated, some

thing floating on the table, some iceberg or island, its sweetness restoring

us, the seconds, minutes, years lost, the burnt sugar's carbon

smell, the cake's walls caving in—form as destiny, how to restore it—

every cake is a failure to sustain joy, a lost place to shelter in, why didn't we

climb it, place a flag at the top instead of these flames' brief banquet.

Notes

The epigraphs cite Natalie Diaz, "The First Water Is the Body," in *Postcolonial Love Poem* (Minneapolis: Graywolf, 2020), 52; and W. S. Merwin, "Witness," in *Migration* (Port Townsend: Copper Canyon, 2005), 286.

"These things that live by perishing" (p. 3), dedicated to Enrique Martínez Celaya, was written partially in response to his show *SEA, SKY, LAND: towards a map of everything* at the Fisher Gallery, University of Southern California, January 19–April 9, 2022.

"Reckless to the Point of Elegance" (p. 24) refers to Francis Bacon's *Study of a Bull* (1991), oil, aerosol paint, and dust on canvas, 198 x 147.5 cm, Guggenheim Museum, Bilbao.

"Brief and unlasting" (p. 40) provides my rendition of a quote from Homer, *The Iliad*, trans. A. T. Murray (Cambridge: Harvard University Press, 1924), book 13, l. 655. Murray's translation reads "and the black blood flowed forth and wetted the ground."

"Et in Arcadia Ego" (p. 46) refers to Nicolas Poussin's *Et in Arcadia Ego* (1637), Louvre Museum, Paris.

"What is desire?" (p. 55) quotes from Emmanuel Levinas, *God, Death, and Time*, trans. Bettina Bergo (Stanford, CA: Stanford University Press, 2000), 195.

"Luna" (p. 63) is dedicated to the memory of R. H. S.

Acknowledgments

Versions of several of poems appeared in the following journals. Special thanks to their editors.

Adroit: "Avalanche," "Going"

American Poetry Review: "What is desire?," "Incarnadine," "A day, a thousand days, a hundred years," "Astronaut"

Colorado Review: "The time it took"

Conjunctions 81: "Here I am again, working between the edge and center," "October," "These things that live by perishing," "When it happened," "While someone sings the blues," "Wind," "*Yes*"

New American Writing 40: "A Swarm of Patience"

New American Writing 41: "Luna"

Plume: "Between," "For luck," "How long, how bright?"

Revel: "Book," "Toward," "Weight," "White"

Terrain: "Et in Arcadia Ego," "Holiday Inn," "Less Vast Pastoral," "What if ?"

"These things that live by perishing" also appeared in the catalogue Enrique Martínez Celaya. *SEA, SKY, LAND: towards a map of everything* (Berlin: Hatje Cantz Verlag, 2021).

Special thanks to friends— Molly Bendall, Alain Borer, Elena Karina Byrne, Peter Campion, Enrique Martínez Celaya, Diana Clarke, Angie Estes, Forrest Gander, Mitchell Jacobs, Claudia Keelan, David Keplinger, Ron Kroutel, Diane Louie, Claudia Moatti, Donald Revell, Nicole Robinson, David St. John, Meredith Stricker, Jim Stone, and Arthur Sze.

With admiration and thanks to Abigail Chabitnoy for selecting this book, to Mary Dougherty and the design team at the University of Massachusetts Press, and to my inspiring colleagues at the University of Southern California.

JUNIPER
JUNIPER PRIZE FOR POETRY

This volume is the fifty-fifth recipient of the
Juniper Prize for Poetry, established in 1975 by
University of Massachusetts Press in collaboration with
the UMass Amherst MFA program for Poets and Writers.
The prize is named in honor of the poet Robert Francis
(1901–1987), who for many years lived in Fort Juniper,
a tiny home of his own construction, in Amherst.